T0194035

How Do You Let Go?

A mother's story

WINIFRED HOWARD

authorHOUSE

AuthorHouse™
1663 Liberty Drive
Bloomington, IN 47403
www.authorhouse.com
Phone: 1 (800) 839-8640

Published by AuthorHouse 07/14/2020

ISBN: 978-1-7283-6625-8 (sc)
ISBN: 978-1-7283-6624-1 (e)

Library of Congress Control Number: 2020911973

Print information available on the last page.

IN MEMORY OF NIKITAH RENEE MACZUGA FARVER
12-9-1986 to 7-18-2017

You will forever be in our hearts and you will be with us everywhere we go until the day we join you. Every place you have visited and every heart that you touched holds a piece of you. We all remember your amazing spirit and the fun we had with you on your journey of life along the way. Rest in Peace my sweet child, until we meet again.

Love you to the moon and back,
Mom

Contents

PROLOGUE

Losing your child brings an intolerable emotional pain that is difficult to understand, much less work through. Since childhood, writing has always been a way to deal with my feelings and when my daughter passed away the flood gates opened wide! Even though my feelings and emotions regarding Nikitah's death are so raw and fresh I will attempt to tone them down as I convey to you the constant struggles with which I have been plagued.

Although I will share memories from her life, I will try not to bore you with great detail. We will walk together through this land of devastation and pain known to me only as only death. I will share with you the terrific person she was throughout her life and try to convey the healing process that followed her death, leading me to where I am today.

Because each of us grieves in their own way, what might take days or weeks for one person to work through may take a year for someone else to get through. Take whatever time you need as there is no template for grief. There is no defined pattern to grief and we will each grieve in our own unique way so if Aunt Sally is telling you to get over it or Uncle Joe does not understand why you are sad or upset as much as you are, and for such a long period of time, let me tell you that what you are going through is completely normal.

Those are the times, those times spent with the Uncle Joes and Aunt Sallys, that I, personally, need to remove myself from situations to kind of recuperate from the effects of what I am hearing.

If you have been here, you know what I am talking about. I invite you to follow me as I figure out how to deal with my daughter's death. You will be with me when I fall to my knees and when I try to determine why someone with so much life ahead of her was taken so soon and you will see how I learned to cope with my grief. You will also see my plan to help others in her memory begin to unfold and hopefully together we can see the plan working the way it was intended.

Because we each grieve differently, my hope is that this book will help someone see a light at the end of the proverbial tunnel and possibly it might lead you lead through the healing process and who knows, maybe you will be able to find peace.

If my words, in any way, help even one person who is struggling then I feel that I have achieved my goal. Please know that any pain, whether physical or emotional no longer exists after death. That thought is what often allows me to get out of bed and start the day.

We are here today and may be gone tomorrow. While many of us struggle on this side with questions about what lies ahead in the afterlife, try to keep in mind that your loved one is in a better place. I know that might sound like something you have heard before, and maybe it is, maybe in a card, a note, or condolence call you received.

It is, however, my own personal belief and it is what gets me through my daily life. I believe that sickness, pain, and torment do not exist in the afterlife unless a person does something totally unspeakable and vial in his physical time on Earth.

It has been three long years since we lost Nikitah. For the past thirty-six months I have written my feelings and thoughts about the death of my amazing daughter in a journal and today you are reading some of my deepest, darkest thoughts. In this book I will share those thoughts, hoping that you will find even the smallest glimmer of hope reading about my struggles. Maybe in some way you may relate to what I am sharing and you will find the strength to continue on with your own journey. Although this book is not meant to make you weepy or tearful, it could be the result and I apologize for that unless, of course, you find solace in the mere idea that someone else feels the same pain you are currently feeling or have previously felt.

Please know that there will be a time when your tears will be replaced with a smile by the mentioning of your loved one's name and I hope that day will come for you soon. As I paged through photo albums from life as we previously knew it, some pictures brought tears while others brought the most happy and sometime, even whimsical, unforgettable memories of Nikitah. Her beautiful personality showed though with every page I turned. I know that she is watching from the place in which she landed and she laughs when I laugh and she continues to comfort me when I am missing her the most.

CHAPTER 1

THE CALL NO PARENT SHOULD EVER RECEIVE

My phone rang, and it was my son-in-law, "Nikitah is dead," he said. Nikitah is my daughter. I thought it was practical joke, so I squealed, "You are not funny, put her on the phone!" He told me, "It is not a joke, she is in our bed and she is dead. The police and coroner are here, and maybe you should come. I told him, "I am on my way," and hung up. I dialed my husband, Dale's cellphone number and when his voicemail picked up the call. I ended the call and dialed the phone number of the main office where he works. The Secretary answered and I told her what happened, she told me she would go into the plant and find him and he would be straight home. I feel like I remember her asking if there was anything she could do to help me but I am not certain as it is all a blur even until this day.

I do remember going outside the house and waiting for him at the curbside for what seemed like forever until he finally appeared on the road out front. I ran to the car and jumped inside, and he laid on the gas as I called my parents with the terrible news. They were to meet us at Nikitah and my son-in-law, Mike's house. I hung up and called my ex-husband, Niki's dad, and told him the horrific news.

The news was too much of a shock for my parents and they were not able to make it to the house. They took the news so hard and as much as I wanted to be there for them I was dealing with the situation, too, and I was where I needed to be at the moment. The days ahead were certain to be horrible and I became almost robotic. I went through the motions, but only remember bits and pieces. I just could not wrap my head around what was happening. The night before that awful call, she was alive and everything was as it had been before, but on this day she was dead.

At the risk of sounding Cliche', I felt like I was in a bad dream and so desperately wanted to wake up. If I could just somehow jolt myself awake, things could go back to the way they were before this day and maybe I could feel normal again. I was in pain and felt so empty inside.

Nikitah was gone and I remember the first birthday we could not celebrate together was my own, it was so hard not to have her there because she was always there for my birthday. She always put so much thought in to making birthdays and holidays special for me from her childhood on through adulthood until the time she died. Nikitah did her best to make holidays and special occasions happy times for the entire family.

We walked life's path together and she was always a phone call or text message away. After she got married and started a life with her husband we saw less of each other as that is the natural progression of life, but we continued to catch up with each others lives regularly. We laughed, we cried, we debated the point, but we always said our 'I love yous' before we went to sleep.

People say the dumbest things for lack of something better to say. I know that grief is a delicate subject for everyone; the person who has lost someone, as well as the individual determining what to say in the moment that they come in contact with the grieving person. A good rule of thumb for someone who is not sure what to say might be to say a simple, " I am sorry for your loss," and leave it at that. Refrain from asking questions about the mechanics of the death; how, why, and when are not necessary and might only add to the stress for the grieving person, and let me tell you there is more stress than anyone can fathom and let's face it, you are only asking out of pure nosiness.

The grieving person is likely distraught over this significant loss and might very well have been crying since the day the death occurred, so nosey questions and dumb comments about your perspective on the situation are only going to make matters worse. In my experience with grief, I would rather people had said nothing as opposed to making me more upset and setting themselves up to look like fools. Even after reading this book, there are people who might say something dumb as opposed to choosing to say nothing at all.

I try so hard to not be offended by people when they do not know what to say so they say whatever comes to mind, no matter how ridiculous it is. I have heard things ranging from, "Was it cancer, drugs, or maybe suicide," to my all time favorite, "The reason I was not publicly crying was that I was always cold hearted and my lack of tears in front of the world proves that I am still the same cold hearted person," WOW! No matter how hurtful the words are, I will not hold a grudge even though, I lack feeling, remember! Let me tell you that I will always turn the proverbial other cheek and let them hit me again, but at some point, watch out!

Nikitah passed away, but I am still her mother. I will continue to support her beliefs and to be strong for her memory and I will attempt to be strong for myself as my life progresses. Each day I must look for a reason to get up, a reason to continue on without her, and a reason to smile again. Nobody that has not gone through the loss of a child has any idea what it feels like, so excuse me if I step on your toes; ignore the previous statement, maybe your toes need some stepping on! This was my daughter, she will always be my daughter, and I will always be her mother. If you do not have kind words, I respectfully ask that you get off your perch and let me grieve in peace.

By the way, for those of you who feel grief is a short process I am guessing you never had reason to grieve and am happy for you, but know that I will likely grieve for the rest of my life because my daughter is no longer there for me to reach out to. She is no longer there for me to ask about her day, or to tell her about my day, or even to argue with. If I had been given a choice to sacrifice my own life so that hers could go on, I would have immediately signed on the line.

We expect to lose grandparents, aunts, uncles, parents, siblings, spouses, and even pets. With exception to terminal illnesses, we never anticipate the loss of our children. It is absurd that this pain, the most unbearable and sometimes even debilitating pain, is supposed to be a normal part of living. I, personally, do not know how that works. Some days I feel as though I am on an amusement ride that spins out of control and the more it spins me around the sicker I become. I just want it to stop and let my life go back to normal but I feel stuck on this ride that seems to have no end in sight. I wonder, *"Is this what the rest of my life will be like?"*

I am a firm believer that God will not give us more than we can handle, but I think I am at that threshold now. So why must I be alive? Some days I wish I were not here struggling with the pain and emotion of losing my child. Every second of every day my heart hurts and I want to see Nikitah or share something about my life with her. Some days I wake up in a state of despair, the sadness envelopes me and my whole day is like one tailspin after another. I keep going round and round but never come to a complete stop. Each day something triggers the memory of that horrible day when I got that call and heard those horrible words, "Nikitah is dead," and I sob without end for a little while.

It could be a picture of her or a photo of a vacation we took, heck it could be a note she wrote to me or a sticky note she left to remind me of something I promised to do, a note she may have written when she was much younger, maybe eight or ten, and it gets me reminiscing about our times together, or it could be a memory of something past that makes me think of her. That one instance plays over in my mind like a vinyl record with a scratch that repeats many times.

Sometimes my mind works around those triggers,and other times they trap me in a place that is very uncomfortable. I think we may be programmed that way, otherwise I would go crazy. My thoughts and the scenario of that awful day would replay in my head forever.

Some nights I jerk awake with that 'punched in the gut feeling,' the feeling that is the same one that I felt at that exact moment when I saw my beautiful thirty-year-old daughter laying there, dead in her bed, knowing that we would never have mother-daughter time again and I would never feel her touch. I questioned in my own mind so many times how this happened. I could not understand how God, my God, the God who I was taught throughout my entire life loves me could allow this to happen. How could my God who is supposed to watch over me, and carry me when I can no longer carry myself take my daughter at such a young age?

I began revisiting the teachings from my years in church and Sunday school. I started to look for answers from the days I taught Bible School to children in our community. I taught those kids about a loving God and I was now questioning if everything taught to me and everything I taught to those children was all wrong.

I sought answers from my Bible for a long time, weeks and months, and eventually, it would be an entire year of questioning, but I unfortunately, came up empty. Everything I read led me to a God who loves us and who wants the best for us and a God who looks out for us, not a God of spite or of revenge. I screamed out, *Why was Nikitah taken from me?* I screeched, *"Tell me why you did this, you should have took me!"*

Back to the day I got the call, I must have been in shock because I felt like I was somewhere else. I called her father and asked that he provide me with any photos of her and that he meet us at the funeral home to go over the arrangements. The entire family struggled through the next days and those days which turned into weeks and if you guessed that those weeks led into months you were right and they were long and difficult months. She passed away on July 18, 2017, five months before her thirty-first birthday and still, today I wait for her to walk through the door and show me something she has been working on.

Nikitah possessed an undying love for her family and was an extraordinary young woman with what I thought would be a wonderful life and bright future ahead of her and now that life was taken from her and she was taken from us. Nikitah had three college degrees and was working on her Master's Degree. She was planning on being a Therapist to help people overcome obstacles in their way of a happy and successful life.

From a very young age Nikitah loved to learn, and she gave learning everything she could from studying subject matter to studying people. She worked as a waitress at the local steakhouse during her last year of high school and into college until they closed their doors, she then worked as a bookkeeper in a specialty restaurant for awhile and when she met her husband they were college students working in the computer department at the university as technicians. After she earned her degree in Computer Information, she began fixing computers in her home during whatever spare time she had. No matter how busy she found her life to be, she always found time to spend with her family.

I am not angry at God for taking her as much as I am disappointed in the way she was treated by some people during her life. I raised her to be strong and independent. She had all of the skills needed to care for herself if I were to die before she was an adult. She could cook and sew by age ten. I remember when she was in third grade we went to stores and she asked me to buy her things but the money was not there and her response, "Use the MAC (Money Access Center) card mom, money is always there."

I knew then she needed to gain more money skills and although she did that very well managing her allowance, it was not enough. When we got home I sat down with her, showed her my checkbook, and explained how it worked. I took the stack of bills out and showed her, explaining that they were all paid every month. I pointed out the due dates and how to know what was due for each. I explained that the money is what I earned by going to work every day. I thought we were done and was returning it to my purse when she said, "Let me do your money, you know I could."

I agreed because I thought she would soon tire of it thinking about paying bills, as I often do, I mean what nine year old manages a checkbook anyway and likes it? I wrote the entries in the log each month and she did the math. I rechecked her work and at the end of the month if there was money left, Nikitah could buy something she wanted as long as it was within reason. It was a good learning experience for her and it was more mommy and me time for us to share, so I guess it was a double reward for the amount of time we spent on it. We were both content, me because I was teaching her a lesson that would carry her through her life and her, because she felt responsible.

My discontentedness is for people who treated her in reprehensible ways and expected me to look the other way, people who would come to me with hugs and make as if they just loved her so much after hearing of her death. I am not saying Nikitah was a perfect person; none of us are perfect and we all learn as we go, honing our skills a bit more with each day. I feel that life is a giant learning curve and somewhere along the way we will all learn that skill which needs to be gained, I just hope it is not to late for some people.

There are people in this world who rarely say anything nice about others unless there is a payoff for them, maybe something the other person can do in return, or maybe the notoriety felt by telling other people of the good deed that they have done. I always categorized them as 'fair weather friends', the friends who like you when things are going good and you are providing something they need; help or an act of kindness. These people are the ones who act as though you are their best friend until something happens that rubs them the wrong way, you are no longer friendship material and they talk about you to anyone that will listen.

Nikitah was the person who turned the other cheek metaphorically. She said what she needed to say, and then she walked away. Sometimes she would stay at a distance until she tested the water and then sometimes things would return to normal. For some of the people in her life that was not the case. In this particular situation, there was a conflict and Nikitah was tagged out until the day she died.

When a particular individual saw my husband and I in the community a point was always made to ask him about his daughter who really did not even know the person, but never asked me how Nikitah was or what she was doing in her life. This individual knew Nikitah from her birth until her death and this passive-aggressive nature of this persons personality must have thought not asking about her would in some way hurt Nikitah, but truth be told,the juvenile behaviors of the adult intentionally aimed at my child hurt me; I was the one who cried myself to sleep at night. So many times my husband and I discussed this person's behavior and how offended we were by it. We made a plan and it was that the next time the situation came up one of us would say, "Nikitah is still living, too, and she is well" and thank them for asking.

Although the situation came up many times after our decision to call it out, we maintained the silence because we would not disgrace ourselves by being so petty and juvenile as this person was. That is water under the proverbial bridge, Nikitah died before that issue could be resolved by the person whose behavior was so deplorable. I question, with that unresolved, *Was that part of God's plan? I know God takes care of things when we meet him and maybe penance is already in order as part of the master plan.* Maybe it will be relationships at work or failed personal relationships. God always works it out.

Nikitah would not want me to hold a grudge as that was not how she rolled and I try really hard not to be that way either, but that was my child the person was disrespecting! I will forever be her mother and I will forever defend her, even if only in memory. If somebody were to say something directly to me that was unacceptable and negative about Nikitah, I might need to roll them over a few times, but for now what is done is done and it is all part of the past so it is time to move forward.

I assume it might be easier for some people to say nice things about a person after they die as, maybe in their mind, that five seconds of kindness makes everything right. I could argue that it does not make anything right, it only made things worse! That was behavior usually engaged in by thirteen- year-old girls, in no way is that adult behavior. It simply rubs salt into the already painful wound.

Maybe saying nice things after someone dies eases the conscience in some way. Each behavior we engage in brings some type of payout, whether it be consequence or reward. There is, however, no reward in fighting with a dead person. If you are fighting with the living, there is always the chance you might be right and you gain some sense of satisfaction in sitting on your perch and feeling that you have won, but a person who fights with the memory of a dead person will surly lose. If the person is deceased, there is no WINNING no matter how high and comfortable you perch might be!

My daughter is gone and nothing will bring her back. There are those days that I still dial Nikitah's number or begin an email or a text to her and then catch myself so I stop, cry about it, and force myself to complete the task at hand so I can go about my day.

I know she is never coming back and I know I will never wish her a happy birthday or give her another Christmas gift or even feel her kiss me and wrap her arms around me as we say goodbye when we part ways after a visit.

The stages of grief do not seem to apply here, there was no bargain to be made. My daughter died at home in her bed and her body was taken from that bed after a full examination. That was the last time I would see her before she was taken to the coroner's office for autopsy and when that was complete she was taken directly to the funeral home from where she would be sent to the crematorium. The wonderful memories of a life that ended too soon is all I have left. I would have gladly died in her place if I had known it were happening; my life is half over and hers had just begun. Although I talk to her every day as I am getting out of bed or motoring about the house, surviving one more day without her, I will never hear her say she loves me again. I would even be happy to hear her make her point about something I said that did not make sense to her.

Nikitah was an intelligent and beautiful young woman who knew exactly what she wanted in life and stood strong and steadfast in her beliefs. She completely owned who she was and she would not allow anyone to get her off track.

Every single day I talk to her not knowing if she can hear me and yet hoping she feels my love wrapping her like a baby swaddled in a soft warm blanket. I think to myself, if she can hear me and does anything I say have any meaning to her at this point? I love her so much and I miss her more with each passing day.

People search for something to say when they see me in the community. They often start the conversation with something like, "I saw the newspaper and I am sorry for your loss." That is acceptable and that alone would be enough to give me the idea that the person was thinking about me.

The day Niki's obituary ran in the paper the telephone rang and I answered to hear a voice of someone I have not seen in years. She was offering her condolences and before the conversation ended the caller asked, "So is it too early to ask how she died?" Part of me wants to say, "My God yes, she only died just yesterday," but I chose to say that I did not know any more than the person asking knew at the time because the autopsy was not yet in.

My brain was in hyper-drive I was fielding phone calls offering condolences and asking if I needed anything. I honestly cannot tell you, even today, three years later what was happening in my mind for at least a month after her death; maybe I cannot remember much of what occurred after her death as a result of some coping mechanism built into my brain. I am slowly regaining little snippets of my memory as it relates to that time in my life.

People say things like,"Time heals all wounds," and they tell me it will be okay. At those times I know people are lost for words and they are trying to comfort me, even though it brings little comfort to me at the time. While I am hearing those words my mind is wondering down a dark path and I say to myself, "*What kind of moron originally came up with those words, because they are pure baloney! I know I have heard those words in songs and maybe even saw them in a sympathy card somewhere along the way but everything will never be okay again*". I understand that as time moves forward the pain I feel will lessen, but my heart will still hurt in the same way, knowing that I will not physically touch Nikitah just one more time, I will never hear her voice, and I can never get another hug from her.

I know I am rambling now, but maybe it is because the pain is so raw, like a knife repeatedly stabbing my heart, so please bear with me as you might be having similar feelings related to your own loss. I have had people say, "I was sorry to hear about your loss," and give me a hug or offer help and that is comforting to some degree. It is when people say things like, "I know how you feel I lost a dear friend several years back," which would have sufficed, except for that as the conversation progressed I found out that the loss we were speaking of was a friend moving away in grade school forty-five years prior.

The person continues on with some jabber that by which point I had completely have tuned out. I just wanted to scream something about the memory of a friend in kindergarten moving away was not anywhere near losing my daughter, but I pressed back the urge. My mind was wondering if she was transported from another galaxy and then I realized she was at a loss and she felt the need to say something to make me feel better so I nodded in agreement.

Nothing makes sense anymore and so many things throughout the day remind me of Nikitah. Each room in the house brings a fond memory of Nikitah from notes she wrote me throughout her life, to pictures of her that adorn my walls, the beautiful comforter she made as a gift to me that keeps me warm each night, and the stuffed animal she brought to me when I was hospitalized, as well as the trinkets she bought me every time she took a trip.

Each and every memory is bittersweet in that I have the warm thoughts attached to each individual item coupled with the sadness and pain of knowing that I will not ever hear her tell me she loves me or feel her embrace as she hugs me before we go our separate ways at family gatherings.

Nobody knows how many creek beds I could fill with the tears I cry in a single day. Some days I cry until my head feels like it is ready to explode. I miss her so much and I do not know how people survive losing more than one child in the same disastrous event.

CHAPTER 2

THE LOSS

One minute everything seems right with the world but then the telephone rings. It is the call that will turn the world as you know it on its side. For me, that call was the worst call I ever received. It was a call that shattered our entire family's world. Hearing that Nikitah was dead was like a blow to the stomach; it was like a terrible nightmare from which I could not awake, and I pray nobody else needs to feel this pain.

As it replays in my mind over the course of time so many questions come to mind; questions for which I have no answers. Questions about how and why it happened flood my mind. I often question if her doctor, who was well aware of issues with her heart rate and blood pressure, would have sent her for tests might I still have my beautiful daughter?

I know that she was gone before I answered the call and yet each time the phone rings I become tense as if there is another awful event on the horizon. In my mind, I somehow relate catastrophe to the telephone ringing and while I know the two are not related my body tenses up and I become filled with anxiety, especially when I am away from home.

The day I answered that call it felt like someone threw a blanket over my face leaving me in complete darkness; I felt like I was being smothered and I could not get a full breath of air. She and I had just sent texts back and forth about a book I wrote that would be in my mailbox the next day and I told her she would get the first copy. She congratulated me, said she was proud of me, and told me she loved me, said we would talk the next day, and we said goodnight, I put the

13

phone down, and went to sleep The next time I would have any phone communication from her home was when her husband, Mike, called to inform me that she had passed in her sleep the next day.

There was an obituary to write, calls to make, decisions to be made, a funeral director to meet with, and the phone rang almost non-stop with condolences, not to mention a plethora of questions, and the list goes on. Somehow we are getting through it one day at a time but I remember little of the happenings of those days after that horrible call.

Everything in the upcoming days was surreal and I was almost robotic, simply going through the motions without fully knowing what I was doing. I guess I had to be cognizant on some level, because everything that needed to be done managed to be completed. The obituary was written, phone calls were made, and I was exhausted.

I guess I was kind of in overdrive, knowing there was so much to be done and this was my daughter so I wanted it to be done right because this would be the last thing I would do for her. The only thing I forgot to do was put her work history in the obituary. I had like six hours to get the obituary written and to the funeral director I put her schooling and her family members and that she passed peacefully in her sleep but I somehow forgot some important information.

There were days throughout this process, and even still today, that I question whether it was worth continuing on with my own life, but as the days continue, so too must living. Scenes from the day I answered the call keep running through my mind and on those days I am more weepy than others. I might see something on television that brings a memory of her childhood and I go off on an emotional expedition. Sometimes, the memory starts with a short burst of tears and moves to remembering many warm memories of her childhood. It usually brings a smile to my face and a warm feeling to my heart, but in a New York minute, I begin to sob uncontrollably, thinking how much it hurts that she is not physically here anymore. If it were simply one thought I might cry a bit and be able to quickly move forward, but unfortunately on some days that one thought brings on a tidal wave of memories and emotions that consume my mind for the rest of the day or maybe longer. Those are the days that make coping the most difficult, days that I often wish that I did not wake up at all.

The phone call from my son-in-law repeats over and over in my head as if it were in a loop, and each time it does, I relive those same feelings that I felt at that very moment. In the weeks after Niki's death, I felt as if I were in a terrible recurring nightmare from which I just could not wake. Albeit less intense, that feeling is still present today and I just want to wake up and have it be a few years ago when everything was normal and life was content and happy for our family. I know that will never happen so I ask myself why I have been left behind, she was a nicer person than me by far and she should be the one still living.

During a situation like this when someone you love passes away you go through certain emotions that are called stages of grief. You may go through each of them in order or you may bounce back and forth, missing a few along the way. Some people do not even go through the stages at all; in any form. Shock is the first stage identified followed by denial, anger, bargaining, depression, and acceptance.

The healing process for every person is different depending on how each of us moves through the stages of the grieving process. I do not tend to fixate on one area over another but I could easily focus on being angry at people who mistreated my daughter at some point during her life, angry at the doctor for not making a proper diagnosis in time to save her life, angry with God for not answering my prayers the way I wanted him to, or I could be angry at myself for not noticing that she was that ill.

I beat myself up for awhile for not seeing just how ill she truly was and, quite often, I still do. I was there for every scraped knee, issues with boys, school deadlines, and anything else that needed my help. From the day she was born I always told her that I would always be there for her and I was. This one time when I missed how sick she was is when she needed me most and I was not there. This time there was no way to make it right and I hope she can forgive me. Part of my training was as a Grief Counselor and while I understand the mechanics behind coping with circumstances and grieving, it is often difficult to follow the advice I might have given to a client. Grief is not carbon copied and the healing process should not be either.

Because grief is so different for each person, the healing process the healing process should be tailored to fit the individual who is grieving.

My period of mourning might be longer or shorter than your period of mourning. One person with the same loss might work through it and move forward with his/her life quicker than another person who is grieving for the same loved one.

For me learning to accept life without my daughter has been challenging and knowing that she would want me to keep living and enjoy what life I have left, might be what compels me to keep moving forward. In my heart, I know that Nikitah is with me and our love for each other remains intact. This may sound silly, but I feel her and sometimes I think I can hear her laugh when I do something absurdly stupid. Right now I feel her presence as I am writing this book and I think maybe she will help me remember everything I need to write. Unlike the obituary which has missing pieces, maybe she will help me include everything that is necessary and get it in the right order.

She was an avid reader and she loved to write so I am sure when I am short on words or cannot get my thoughts on the paper she is right beside me guiding me through the process. I miss her so much and I often begin to dial her phone number only to realize that her phone number has been reassigned to someone else, so I disconnect the call and put the phone down before dialing the last digit.

Even though I can not physically hear her speak via the telephone I lay the phone down and I talk aloud to her. I talk like if I were on the phone with her as if we are having a conversation and at those times, I wish I could hear her speak back. When I am changing the bed linens or making the bed I am talking to her about the beautiful comforter, pillows, and curtains she made for meas a Christmas gift one year. When I am tidying up I talk about the trinkets she bought for me, and other times I talk about whatever comes to mind, maybe just to feel like I talked to her each day like I did when she was alive.

During the weeks directly following her death I told her that I was upset that she left me and that I would never understand what happened. I told her that I love her and that she will always be the light in the darkness for me. Now, I talk to her throughout the day.

I miss our walks together and talking about whatever we wanted to talk about for however long we felt like we had the energy to keep talking and walking. I used to tell her that she was like my own personal trainer when we walked and told her, "A paid trainer would not push me so hard," at that time she would usually find a hill for us to climb. Even though she pushed me so hard,I would do it all again. I would give anything to relive those times.

We would do as many as thirty-nine miles in three or four after work walks. When I would tell her I was too tired to keep going she would point to a hill we would walk it, heck sometimes it felt like we almost trotted up it. Today I am lucky if I can walk two or three town blocks before my legs quit moving, but I am thinner as a result of Nikitah's efforts. When push came to shove she was always there for me and I tried to be there for her.

Niki always helped me when I had problems with my computer, she tutored me with algebra when I needed it to finish my licensing, she helped me with things around the house,even after she was married and had a home of her own. In my eyes, she was simply an amazing person!

I guess Mitch Albom knew what he was talking about when he said, "Death ends a life, but not a relationship," and I think he was right. Death was the end of her natural life, but our relationship still holds strong. Those words ring true for me as death might have taken Nikitah from us, but it did not take the relationships we had with her. We are still her loving family; she has a husband, parents, grandparents, aunts, uncles, cousins, and siblings who love and miss her. We all miss her so much.

Sometimes, especially when I am home alone or driving in the car, I find myself asking, "Niki, do remember when we all went on that beach trip," and I talk aloud about what fun it was or maybe I talk about an event in her life that was important like her confirmation a special birthday party, the day she met her soulmate, Mike, or how happy they both were on their wedding day. While I cannot hear her answer, I am positive she hears me because I sense her presence. I think about those wonderful times and the memories we made along the way often and, yes, at times I cry. I am not totally without emotion.

My life changed in an unimaginable way as a result of her death and it will never be the same. Although my pain of losing Nikitah will lessen over time, I will grieve the loss of her for the rest of my life and it will be a glorious day when we are reunited upon my own death.

CHAPTER 3

UNFATHOMABLE PAIN

When Nikitah died it was like a huge black fabric fell down on me and wrapped around me. My breathing was constricted and I felt numb and almost hollow, not in a physical sense but in a mental sense. I was like a robot. I was doing everything that needed to be done, but I was not necessarily aware I was doing it.

First there was disbelief and then at her at her home I hurried out of the car and ran inside the house where I was questioned about what might have occurred; things like did she get along with her husband, did she ever confide any domestic abuse, did she drink or use drugs, and the list goes on. I know it was all part of the process, but it was draining and monotonous.

The emergency responders kept going in and out of the bedroom where she lay each time closing the door behind them. Finally, they told my husband and I we could go in. We stepped inside and I saw her laying in that bed, eyes open and smiling. She was reaching for something and the smile on her face gave me a sense that she saw something or someone familiar and she was not afraid.

Still in shock, I leaned down, kissed her, and said, "I love you my beautiful baby," then I told her, "Your Gram and Pap love you too and you are now and forever with us all". I stepped back so Dale could have time with her. The whole thing was surreal and maybe even eerie; it was like something right off of an episode of Law and Order. There was a police officer watching from behind us and another behind him and

I felt like a suspect, and I guess at that time maybe I was, heck maybe everyone in the room was.

We turned and headed back into the living room where there were more questions from the police officers and the Deputy Coroners. Then I saw them bring the gurney and I knew I needed to go home. I told the officer that I could not watch my daughter taken out in a bag and if he had more questions he had my phone number. He nodded his head in agreement, handed me his card, and told me to call him if I needed to talk or thought of anything I forgot to tell him; I reached for Dale's hand and we left.

I do not remember crying on the way home, I remember feeling numb and empty. It was so quiet on the trip back to the house; there was no radio and we did not talk. When the car stopped in front of the house I just sat there until Dale came around to my side, opened the door, and helped me out of the car. As I got out I it was difficult for me to put one foot in front of the other. He took my arm and helped me onto the porch and through the front door. When we got inside I dropped onto the sofa and stared at the wall in front of me. Photos of Niki's life adorned that wall: a cruise we went on, pictures of her with family members, photos with friends she met along the way, along with her wedding photos, and many more memories.

Some people think the tears should be over and that enough time has lapsed to end the grieving process, but I am here to say that grief does not work that way. I cannot tell you how long I will continue to cry or what is customary but I can say that I honestly do not care what anyone thinks. Each person is unique in their characteristics and traits and each of us grieves in our own way and for whatever amount of time we find necessary to help us in the healing process. Some people may not completely heal for a variety of reasons.

My maternal grandmother died more than forty-five years ago and my mother still grieves the loss, albeit not as often as it was right after it happened, she still cries at times when she remembers something special about her mother and she still misses her. I know that I will cry for Nikitah as long as I am alive and my memory holds.

Nikitah and I were so close and shared so many memories that I might cry on and off for the rest of my life, who knows. I miss her each and every day. We were walking partners, sounding boards, confidants, and much more. Nikitah and I had a strong bond, we supported each other. For twenty years, we were all each other had and during those years we relied on each other a lot. She depended on me for almost everything as a child, but as she became more independent it seemed to level out and we both looked to each other for support. We could disagree or bicker about things in the morning, but when the day was done we were mother and daughter and we always knew how much love there was between us.

Some people think I do not cry enough, one person even referred to me as being cold- hearted, imagine that being said the day after my daughter died, simply because I was not a fountain of tears in front of everyone, I was still in shock! Those words ripped a hole in my heart that only started to mend a year or so ago. There are many tears for Nikitah every single day, they just are not on a billboard for everyone to see. Usually, I cry in the privacy of my home where I do not need to answer questions about why I am crying. I should not need to make anyone understand what is happening, I am crying simply because I feel the need to cry. As I am writing this book I break down so many times, my face gets all twisted up, and the abysmal crying begins with lots of tears and no end in sight. There have been times that felt like I might have damaged a blood vessel by one eye or the other because my face was swollen and red by the corner of my eyes and they stung around the corners. It all cleared after I took time to rest and used a cool compress for a bit.

As a Grief Counselor I often helped people deal with loss and part of my training taught me that when we cry we are not crying for the person we lost, we are crying for ourselves and I often used that as a tool to help people understand that the person who has passed no longer has sickness or pain. I also explained the traps and triggers that keep them where the are and do not allow them to move forward in the healing process. I shared with them my own losses throughout the years and felt confident in my skills, working diligently to get them to the next step in the process in an attempt to find healing. Today I can tell you most of that is hogwash, it is something you say to help someone through the difficult time they are they are experiencing and if it helps anyone, just one person, that is wonderful but the reality of death and grief is that each of us must deal with it in our own way.

While I understood that loss is difficult, I never truly had a grasp on the whole grief process until Nikitah died. I am not crying for her as a result of any pain she could be in because there is no pain where she has gone. I am crying for her because of how much I miss her. And how much I need her here with me to continue our life's path. We were not done sharing our lives and she was taken from me!

While the trainings I participated in as part of my licensing requirement as a Grief Therapist helped prepare me to help those who experienced losses, they did not prepare me to find my way through my own grief. One thing that was said in those trainings was spot on! They drummed into my head that the grieving person cries for himself because of the emptiness the person has been left with after death and as a result of the roller coaster of emotions that are being experienced throughout the grieving process. It is true, in reality, I am crying for me because a piece to my life puzzle is missing and I realize that no matter how much I might look, it will never be found during this lifetime.

I cling to the hope that there is an afterlife where we will be reunited and find our 'happy ever after'. Around 400 BC, Plato spoke of the Cyclical Theory of Life where if a person was good in his mortal life he would have a good afterlife and if he were bad in life, he would suffer and be tormented in the afterlife, much like the Bible describes Heaven and Hell. The main difference, in my mind, was that Plato also believed that after a thousand years or so the dead person would recycle and be born as someone else with no recollection of his previous life. I guess that could be recycling at its finest. The Bible states that the damned will go to Hell and the righteous will go to Heaven to await the Revelation.

I know that I will see Nikitah again and I anxiously await that day when we are reunited, but until then, I will make the best of this life that I am currently living.

CHAPTER 4

PEOPLE DO NOT UNDERSTAND

I spent nine months talking to the life growing inside of my belly, telling my baby that I would always love it and be there in good times and in bad. On that cold day on December ninth back in 1986, I became a mother. When my baby was brought to me in the hospital I knew that the role God blessed me with was the most important role of all, for now, I was a mommy. I was not just a woman, a daughter, or a wife, but now I was a a mother, and I knew that no matter what would happen for the rest of our lives, my role as Nikitah's mother would supersede my own needs.

Just four months after her birth, we experienced our first life changing event when I left my husband and our life situation changed. During that time of uncertainty about what the future held, I knew we would make it because there was no other choice. That was a life altering situation but I knew we would get through it.

I had a life other than my own to support and protect and I planned to give Nikitah everything I could. I pushed my own needs to the background so her needs were always met. I returned to school and got an education so I could provide for her. I wanted to give her the best life I could with everything she would need to be successful. Between her daddy, me, and her grandparents, Nikitah had a wonderful childhood and not one true need ever went unmet, leaving her with many good memories. After her death I realized that all of the efforts I made early on in her life might have provided security and a sense of well-being but in the end, death won.

Niki's death was the life altering blow that shattered my world. It changed the course of my life and I was now thrown into a complete sensory overload each time something or someone reminded me of her. Because it was her and I for so long, we had so many good memories and when I see something that reminds me of one of those times I experience an eruption of tears much like an active volcano erupting and spewing hot lava on everything in sight.

We were close and we were able to rely on each other as a source of support whether it be emotional or just by being there. We were only a mere phone call apart any time one of us needed a shoulder or someone to dump on. We laughed and cried together, we joked, we talked about life, and at times, we argued about dumb stuff, but at the end of the day we loved each other so much.

From childhood on, Nikitah and I always said we loved each other at the end of the evening when we said our good-nights. We made a rule to never go to bed angry at each other, even if it meant sorting everything out into the early morning hours. Some days our "Good nights," would be at four A.M., I guess that kind of made them "Good mornings".

CHAPTER 5

A NORMAL GRIEVING PERIOD?

What is a proper amount of time to grieve the loss of someone you love so much? In the work world you typically get bereavement days to grieve the loss of a loved one after their death. The typical amount of bereavement days depend on the type of work you do and the company's policy. I find myself questioning who determines the number of days that are permissible. Has the person making the rule ever lost anyone they loved and how long did it take to get over it.

Do you get over a loss of such magnitude as the loss of your child? I do not have a clue. But I can say that grief is not short term. It is something you live with in your daily life. Each and every day grief presents itself at different times in different ways. For me, personally, I may see someone who reminds me of her and if I do not approach with caution it can have a bad outcome. On the flip side, if I set my mindset at a place where I can look away or say hello with a smile make like I am in a hurry, and simply walk away the outcome can be much different.

If someone were in a state of shock after a death, much like I was, those first three customary grieving days might not be as difficult as the days and weeks that follow. It had been eighteen months since Niki's death and it still felt raw and new, like it happened just the week before. While I can go out with friends and I have started doing some of the things I enjoyed before her death. I continue to set an intention for the day, a positive plan,in hopes that if I stick to it the day will be a good one. My intention for one Friday was not to cry because Nikitah is in a place where pain and sickness do not exist and I know we will be reunited again one day. I made it until about 11:00 A.M. before the tears ran down my face and dripped to the floor. I turned the music up and went about my chores. Everything was going as planned and I was dancing around with my vacuum in hand. Out of nowhere I was crying and missing Nikitah so much. I grabbed a tissue, reminded myself of my intention, and continued to clean.

Within a few minutes a song Nikitah always played when she lived at home, a song by her favorite artist, came on the radio and I began to cry again. I remember that as my eyes welled with tears I thought about how much Nikitah loved that song and the fact that she was probably hearing it with me and she was likely singing and dancing too. The entire weekend was similar in that it was filled with memories, reminders of having her here, as well as lots of good memories and many tears. Not to worry though, those tears are necessary for the healing process and they are reminders of happy times. Many of my tears seem to be transitioning from tears of sadness to those that are full of good memories.

I still continue to set my intention for the day every morning but no matter how good my intention may be, sometimes my grief finds a back door to sneak in to throw everything out of whack. I do everything in my power to get back on my game, sometimes I find my way back to an even plane quickly and other times I cry on and off for a great portion of the day.

When someone says you should be over it or you need to get back in the saddle, it has been a week, a month, or even a year. I cringe. My question to them would be, "How do you come up with such stupid ideas?" The two or three days you might be given off work that are bereavement days are, in my mind, a starting point as they give you time to meet with funeral home, set arrangements in place, maybe fit in the service, and get back to work.Even upon returning to work, you will struggle to cope with pain and the residual feeling of emptiness that is left by the death of a loved one.

If or when you go back to work you will undoubtedly face the coworkers who mean well but have questions or offer to be there if you need them. That is all well and good, but those same people bring it up on a routine basis maybe because they are nosey or maybe they truly do care and are not sure what to say in the situation.

Some people think the crying should be done but I am sure I will cry throughout my life. I miss her each and every day. We were walking partners, sounding boards, confidants, and that strong bond we created could not be dissolved, even by death. We could disagree or bicker about things in the morning, but when the day was done we were mother and daughter and we always knew how much love was there between us.

Still, other people think I do not cry enough, one person even referred to me as being cold- hearted, imagine that being said the day after my daughter died, simply because I was not a fountain of tears in front of everyone, I was still in shock! Even today, I cry in the privacy of my home. Well, okay, at least I cry privately where I am not seen only to be asked what is wrong.

For so many years it was because of Nikitah that I had a reason to live. When my marriage with her father fell apart, Nikitah was four-months-old and there is something about being a single mother that provides a person with the motivation necessary to survive. Not only was the plan to survive, but to survive well and provide a future for my baby. My parents were a huge part of that and because we lived in close proximity to each other they were very involved in Niki's life on an almost daily basis and I am grateful that they loved her so much.

We went to the beach every summer, sometimes multiple times. Soon the beach became a second home to Nikitah and she could not get enough salt-water and seagulls. It did not matter if we stayed in a small motel or a resort right on the ocean, Nikitah was at her happiest breathing in the salt air.

Some of my fondest beach memories with Nikitah were of staying in a cabin about half an hour from the ocean. I recall that on one particular trip we stayed in a cabin and Nikitah convinced her Grammy to stay at the fire roasting marshmallows and they were up well into the night roasting marshmallows and making S'mores I became bored with it, but Nikitah called it 'Grammy time' and it made her feel special, I am so glad she had that special time.

There were many memories made with both of her maternal grandparents because they were as involved as they wanted to be. If one of my parents would call and ask what we were doing or if we wanted to meet them somewhere we usually made ourselves available. They were very important to Nikitah and she was important to them. Those are the kind of memories you take with you. I never could understand how they could sit at the fire so long, but they had a great time and I heard all about it the next day.

The next morning, she was up and ready to head to the beach with sand molds and shovel in hand waking everyone up. She could not contain her energy and when we got to the beach she grabbed her Pappy's hand and led him toward the ocean where, together, they spread out a blanket . By the time we got to them she had a bucket filled with ocean water and threw it at him, soaking him. Those are the days I love to remember, when life was lived in the current moment. Even as an adult Niki talked about those days at the cabin near the beach.

As an adolescent, Nikitah loved to help her pap work around the house and she even helped him on jobs for his contracting business. She learned quite a bit about the trade and often would fix things at our home growing up. After she married Mike and moved into her own home she was hanging out with me at the house one day and noticed a section of wallpaper that had been scratched by the ca and made mention of it

Before I knew what she was thinking, Nikitah asked if there was extra wallpaper and I told her where to find it. She grabbed the scissors and cut the paper to fit what was needed. As she folded the paper she said, "Watch and learn, you should probably know how to do this." Those were the very words I heard from my dad when he made any repairs at my home or at his own home with my mom throughout the years.

Nikitah wiped out the kitchen sink, filled it with warm water, rolled up the wallpaper, and dropped it in. She took a clean towel out of the kitchen drawer and took the wallpaper to the kitchen table and folded some special way. I thought she was doing Origami or something and seeing my expression she said, You need to book it to do it right, mom,' and she had the damaged wall fixed in no time. Within minutes the wall was made new again. She cleaned up the mess and said, "That's how you fix that problem," rubbed her hands together, and we went out the door to walk. She did yet another good deed for someone else, me, and I was happy the wall was fixed.

Over the course of her life, everything I did whispered her name. I returned to school to further my education so that I could provide her with a better life, saved money to build her inheritance, and now she is gone and I struggle to make it through another day without her.

When she was younger, Nikitah did not like people touching her things, she thought they would be broken. Everything had an intrinsic value and was irreplaceable in her mind and she never threw her dolls on the floor. As a child she placed a high value on her things and she protected them at all costs, even if it meant loss of friendship. As she grew older those things were just that, THINGS, but some continued to have a higher level of importance to her than others, dependent on how she acquired them.. She often came home and rummaged through the attic with Mike to determine what she wanted to hang on to and take others to sell online or at a yard sale. Some of them she gave to others or made a donation to charity.

Nikitah sent money to St. Jude's Children's Hospital, she tutored middle and high school students who struggled in English, Algebra, and History. She especially liked tutoring students who were learning about the Civil War because Nikitah felt that her knowledge of that war could be used to bring it it to life and make anyone want to know more.

I shared the pain of losing her, now let me share the joy of life with her in it. She was imaginative, creative, and kind. She had an abundance of empathy for others, especially those less fortunate than her. That empathy led to helping people in many ways. I chaperoned a field trip to New York City when Nikitah was in seventh grade. Upon coming out of a McDonald's Nikitah and another female student took their bags to a bedraggled man who was sitting at a bench. His button down shirt had tattered sleeves, one of which was torn off. The whole front of the shirt was stained with what looked like coffee or tea. His shoes were worn out and way too big for his feet.and he wreaked of body odor.

Both girls nonetheless walked over and said,"Hi". He looked at them with crazy eyes and said, "Hello". They sat on the bench one of them on each side of the man next to him and opened their bag and one gave the man her french fries while the other gave him her sandwich. I told them how nice that was and offered to replace the food they shared but they chose to share what was left with each other. Nikitah said, "We helped someone else and we still had enough left for us.

The man got up from the bench with his pants falling half way down at the waste and walked toward us. I thought he might ask for a drink but as he walked by he said, "Nice girls." The smell of dirty clothes and perspiration stung in my nostrils, but Nikitah and her friend smiled at him as they bade him a nice day.

Summers were usually busy at our house with her friends hanging out in the pool or being goofballs in the garage. Anytime she thought friends were coming over to hang out with her in the summer she always made sure we had a refrigerator full of drinks and a cabinet full of snacks to share with everyone. If something was missing she would write it on paper and stick it to the refrigerator with a magnet for me to pick up the next time I was at the store.

I never minded Niki's friends being at our house because they were good kids and I knew that everyone was safe. They always had fun and Nikitah usually ended up the one they would put on their shoulders and throw into the pool. Those were the good times, the days of summer with no homework, no obligations, and days that seemed like they lasted forever; they were her days to enjoy. Those were the days to let her light shine, and she did. Summer would soon end and the school year would begin.

Most of the birthdays and holidays fell between the start of school and May. Nikitah loved to shop for people and often spent hours finding the right gifts for birthdays and holidays so the people she loved the most could feel just how much love she had for them. One Christmas after they married, Nikitah and her husband, Mike, brought so many gifts in to the house and piled them by the tree on Christmas morning that there was hardly space to move around the room. I got the plate of snacks ready as I do every year and we sat down waiting for, her grandparents, my mom and dad to come. Because they live only a few blocks away It has been part of Christmas since the day she was born and Nikitah looked forward to spending time with them.

Many of the pajamas and lounge-wear I have were gifts from Nikitah.She always went above and beyond. She knew I liked Winnie the Pooh and she she bought me Winnie the pooh cookbooks and made me a fleece throw accompanied by two travel pillows with Winnie the Pooh on them. I remember one Christmas she had a tablet and pencil and asked me what I wanted for Christmas. I told her that I did not want anything and she said, "Then what do you need?" I told her socks for work. We often played games where she was a waitress of store clerk so each time she asked what I needed I said, "Socks."

I was shocked on Christmas morning when there were thirty- one small packages under the tree for me and four or five larger ones with my name on them. I opened a medium package and got my favorite perfume and then she opened a gift and then my parents, and so on. My second package was a tiny one and I opened it to find two pairs of black trouser socks. I said thank you and the next person opened a gift. My mom got a hair dryer, dad got a power tool, and we kept opening until everything was opened.All in all I opened forty four pairs of socks. I think I still have some of those socks and I would give anything to relive that Christmas morning.

Because Nikitah was fluent in Spanish I would often call her when I got a new family on my caseload who did not speak English very well and she would give me a short course in conversational Spanish or at the holiday when I was going to deliver gifts she would tell me how to say phrases I would need to have a positive interaction with them in the language they are comfortable with.

Let me assure you that I learned every word of the Christmas song, Feliz Navidad by Jose Feliciano that year and I thought I was prepared. I walked up to the house with two boxes filled with presents and a gift card to the local grocery store. I sat the boxes down and went to the car to get two more boxes. I returned to the house and rang the doorbell. The woman answered and I said "Feliz Navidad," as I handed her the envelope with the Christmas card in Spanish and the gift cards. She called for her children to come collect the boxes and take them inside. She became very vocal and her arms began flailing around. She thanked me and told me to go, or so I thought.

I remember calling Nikitah as I left a client home and telling her, "I think I was just told thank you now go!" She asked what the lady said and I told her, "The mother took the gifts and the grocery card and told me, "Gracias (which I knew was Thank You) and Adios (which I thought was good-bye which meant get out of here)!" Nikitah told me that the woman was saying, 'Gracias alabado sea dios,' which is probably misspelled, but it translates to, 'Thanks be to God,' So, then I felt bad that I had just turned around and walked away. Nikitah said I had just done a good deed and helped God's people and she was sure I was going to Heaven.

She did good things behind the scenes that people did not see. Case in point, Nikitah sold cosmetics and the week of Christmas she gave me hand lotions and lip balms that she bought with her discount to use as incentives for my students; there were enough for all of them. She said, "I know you do a behavior modification program and I thought these might be useful,"as she placed them on my sofa. She was a wonderful daughter and I miss her so much!

The pain and suffering left by Niki's death seems endless. Those are the days I feel like I am running in a hamster wheel, with no end in sight and I question why hamsters just keep running when they get nowhere. Maybe they are really into exercise and that wheel is what keeps them fit! Do not misunderstand, I have good days where I smile and laugh, but tears somehow find a way to invade my thoughts on those days as well.

Giving birth to Nikitah was a high point in my life and her death took me to the lowest place I have ever been, a place from which I feared, there may be no return. I ask myself often, *How can I be expected to get through this?"* I have heard that we are put through trials and tests in our lives but I often find myself shrieking, *"Really, how will this benefit anyone, my baby is gone, so does that mean I failed the test?"* This is in fact the most difficult test I have ever taken and I am not sure how I am progressing.

Sometimes when I am home alone, I scream things like, *"I can not take anymore,"* or *"Okay, you win!"* In all honesty, when I think about what I am saying, I feel like I have gone mad, as I am yelling some nonsense about failing and someone else winning, as if I were in some kind of game. This is not a game, it is life, and some days it sucks! Niki's death has affected so many lives. Her life was beautiful and full of promise,but it ended way to soon. Her death changed the lives of her family for as long as we all might live.

It is especially on those days that I often feel like I am running in a hamster wheel; I just keep on going until I am ready to drop into the abyss of sadness and darkness that have become my new normal. Those are the days I feel like I never make progress, nor do I reach the destination toward which I have been moving. The past thirty-six months seem like a repeating loop that never change, forcing me to relive the day I answered that call.

Niki's birth was the high point of my life and her death has taken me to a point from which I fear there may be no return. There were so many wonderful moments throughout her life from birth to death and now I feel like I am stuck in one spot. I am so tried of walking up the down escalator in what feels like high speed. I wish there was a magic potion of sorts for me to drink so that I might be able to reset my life to a better place in time, a time in which Nikitah was healthy and full of life and we were all together again.

CHAPTER 6

HOW DO I HANDLE THIS?

From the second I heard that Nikitah was gone I was in a state of disbelief and when we pulled up in front of her house and saw the police cars and ambulances with lights a blazing it became more real and I could feel my heart sink. We parked the car and as I and I hurried out of the car toward the house house, making my way around what seemed like miles of yellow police tape, finally getting to the bottom step of the porch I felt both, a sense of urgency and doom.

Inside the house, police and coroners questioned us about what might have occurred; things like did she get along with her husband, did she ever confide any domestic abuse, did she drink or use drugs of any type, and the list goes on. When they felt satisfied that they had enough answers to complete the next part of the investigation, they returned to the bedroom where she lay.

They kept going in and out of the bedroom and back to the room where we all sat, each time asking the same questions another time; a third time, and fourth time, I lost track. Finally, they told us we could go in. We stepped inside and I saw her lying in that bed, eyes open and smiling. She was reaching for something and the smile on her face gave me a sense that she saw something or someone familiar and she was reaching for it or heading toward it.

Still in shock, I leaned down, kissed her, and said, "I love you beautiful baby," then I told her, "Your Gram and Pap love you too and you are forever with us all". I stepped back so Dale could have time with her. He leaned down and kissed her; he said something to her as he turned around to leave.

The whole thing was surreal and maybe even eerie. There was a police officer watching from behind us and another behind him. We turned and headed back to the living room where there were more questions from the policemen and the Deputy Coroner.

Then I saw them bring the gurney and I knew I needed to go home. I told the officer that I could not watch my daughter be taken out in a bag and if he had more questions he had my phone number. He nodded in agreement, gave me his card, and told me to call him if we had any questions or remembered anything of importance that might help their investigation. I took the card, shoved it in my pocket, hugged Mike, Dale and I told him goodbye and we left.

I struggle every single day with this grief which has become my daily pattern of living. For a lengthy period of time, my life became a mere existence. Something is wrong in my life and I simply do not have any idea what to do. My daughter is gone and the hole in my heart is so huge that even the best heart surgeon in the world would not be able to fix it.

Somehow, even though that was the most difficult time in my life, things managed to get done and I am not sure how. Looking back, I realized I did not put her work history in the obituary. Nikitah worked as a Computer Technician, a waitress at the local steakhouse, a bookkeeper for a local Italian Restaurant, and tutored students in what time she had left. I did not even think of that missing piece until a month or so later when there was time to reflect on what happened. I was lucky to get her name, date of birth, maternal and paternal family members, and siblings all on paper. Not only did I miss her work experience but also the things she loved to do.

Nikitah and I used to hit up every concert we could when the bands came to our area. It did not matter to us if we were in the front row or sitting in the field, we enjoyed the music and we loved being together. Any local concert from classic rock to country music and everything in between, we were sure to be there. Her love for music became inevitably clear at a Billy Ray Cyrus concert to which my mom and I accompanied her. The clouds opened and poured down on us all night as we sat on the horse track in muddy gravel. Nikitah did not even notice that she was soaked because she was so involved in the performance.

She made a plan for us to see every music artist from A to Z and we worked on it. The list began with Alabama and ended with Trisha Yearwood because ZZ-Top was too much for her. We saw some of her favorites like REO Speed wagon, Foreigner, Journey, and Styx four or five times each and their signed photos were in frames in her bedroom. Forgive me for babbling on, but her life was so full and and she was filled with energy at those concerts. Today, I wonder if she enjoys music where she is and if she is singing along as she always did. Who knows, maybe she hears the music that plays in our house each day and she is dancing and singing along!

Nikitah was also a terrific big sister to her foster siblings, one whom Dale and I later adopted. When Niki went to Governor's School at Penn State University and we went to visit. She grabbed Jofenna's hand and took her over to the Nittany lion and sat there with her so we could get a photo. She always referred to Jofenna as her little sister and she would be proud to know Jofenna's children and call them her niece and nephew.

—————————— CHAPTER 7 ——————————

PEOPLE MAY NEVER KNOW

People may never know the struggle of losing a child and I am happy for them. I wish I did not have such an intimate relationship with death. Being fully aware that tomorrow will be here in what seems like a blink of an eye, and that we are not promised to see that day or any other day for that matter, I enjoy my life as much as is possible but nothing brings me the same joy as seeing Niki's smile or hearing her tell me about an amazing trip they took or about something else awesome in her life. She brought so much completeness to a day simply with her beautiful smile or the hug she gave me just before we parted ways at events or visits. I miss those days and think about them often.

Nikitah was under the weather for some time, but when she spoke to me she would tell me the doctor knew her blood pressure was up and down and that her heartbeat was erratic and he thought it was due to her young age or exercising before an appointment and did not offer medication to combat it or suggest any follow up appointments. She told me some days she was weak and she asked about my diagnosis of Muscular Sclerosis, asking my initial symptoms, telling me that she researched it to see what the genetic risk was to her as my child.

Nikitah did not share much about her health with me except for that she was under doctor's care and hoped to be feeling better soon. I assumed that the doctor would do what was necessary to assure Nikitah's health was on track, after all is that not why there is a Hippocratic oath in which the physician swears to respect the gains of science while treating his patients with respect and dignity but I am not so sure he did that!

I guess the assumption that the doctor would do right was not necessarily correct. At first, I was totally angry at the doctor, so much that I went in to the clinic and had myself withdrawn from his patient list. My fear was that seeing him when I was ill would result in words said, by me of course, that would bring turmoil that neither of us needed and I might even be escorted from the clinic by men in black uniforms with a club and badge.

I have some great days, as great as possible given the situation, and then I have mediocre days, but since Niki's death I continue to live with one hand on the panic button at all times. If something is about to happen, I want to be as prepared as possible the next time. I was blind sided by her death and it was terrible; I never want to feel that way again.

Many times, as a therapist, I was told by people that they spoke to a loved one or saw them in their dreams and someone even told me that her aunt who had passed guides her on her daily path through life. That did not happen with me. The shock of losing my child plummeted me into the middle of a mental state of being where I felt virtually frozen in time. I knew what was happening around me, but could not interact with people and my environment, nor did I feel the need for any interaction.

I felt like my mind stopped and my body was going through the motions much like a television program going on and on with muted sound. I saw people's lips moving, comprehended the bits and pieces I was able to catch, and the rest was a visceral void forcing my mind to feel vacant and lost. I often saw commercials for allergy medicines on television where they talked about someone sitting in a room full of people and feeling like everyone and everything was off at a distance and the person was not there. I often wondered what that must feel like, but unfortunately, I certainly understand that feeling now. It was becoming clear and I thought to myself, " *This must be exactly the feeling they were talking about!*"

Soon the feeling that I was in a void turned to one of despair. I was angered and frustrated by everything! People's actions or in some cases, in-actions appeared to be the culprit. In an effort to work through my grief, I was drawing lines in the sand, which I would not cross, giving myself permission to avoid places and people that would remind me of my loss and allowing myself to put aside my daily tasks whenever I felt the need. I was in a cold and very dark place, maybe you have been there yourself.

About three and one-half weeks after her passing, while soaking in a hot tub in preparation for bedtime, I was reflecting on the wonderful life she had up until death took her away. There were many times during her youth, she would call me when she got home from school just to update me on her day or to ask about my day. A few years later, she would call me to update on college and a variety of other things that were going on in her life, I often received phone calls from her throughout the day when something happened,whether it be good or bad.

I thought about how happy she was on her wedding day and how much she loved her husband, and how he supported her hopes and dreams. They were a wonderful couple and you could feel the love they had for each other when they were near, whether it be running into them at a local carnival, a county fair, or something as simple as a picnic at the house.

I was thinking how abruptly it all came to an end. Thinking about the day she died, I began to sob. The sobbing continued throughout the evening and I am not entirely certain that I actually went to sleep that night but I do remember Dale holding me all night long as I cried. I remember him telling me that he wished he could do more to help me feel better. In my heart I knew that the only way I could feel better was if this never happened. I was envisioning a life where I could simply reset my life back to when Nikitah was alive and everyone was healthy, much like the system restore on the computer that Niki used to do when she had a computer issue, who knows maybe that is what the future holds.

At one point Dale said something like, "It will be okay honey," and I do not remember exactly what I said. My heart was ripped into pieces and at that point and I do remember thinking, *"Nothing will ever be okay again, from the day she was born, Nikitah was always the person who made my world okay and now she is gone."* Even if we were disagreeing about something, simply knowing she was there was what made it all okay.

My eyes were getting heavy and I guess I was all cried out because the next thing I remember was that Nikitah was standing in front of me. She told me, "It is all good mom I feel better than I have felt in a long time. I love you guys, see ya' later," and with that, she rubbed my husband's shoulder and disappeared into the night. That was the first night of sleep I had after her passing for at least nearly four or five weeks.

A few days later I was at my parents' house sitting at the kitchen table and my cell phone rang. I pushed the speaker button and answered the call. Niki's voice was on the line, it was her voicemail message, which my husband saved to my computer at home so I would always remember her voice. We were all shocked and as you can imagine, we talked about that for a long time. We still have no clue how that happened but I believe it was a sign from her letting us know she is with us and that we should not despair. I only wish that I could see her and touch her again, I need a physical hug from her and I need her to whisper in my ear, assuring me that she is at peace.

CHAPTER 8

WHAT TRIGGERS THESE FEELINGS?

For me, grief can be, and is frequently, triggered by almost everything and quite often by what seems like nothing at all. I can be in the mall or at a red light and a commercial on the radio brings up a memory of her being silly or singing along to the jingle.

Every day things bring about thoughts of Nikitah. It could be something little like a song on the radio, a child at the mall that resembles her when she was small, a book written by an author she loved, or I can be sitting in a doctor's office or walking through a store and thoughts of Nikitah just flood my mind, usually followed by uncontrollable weeping. It is unconscionable to me that anyone should ever suffer through the loss of their child and this kind of pain that is often, at times, unbearable.

We all go through life coping with the loss of friends, loved ones, grandparents, other family members, and even pets who many consider to be family members, but those losses pale in comparison to losing your child. Some people are sick for extended periods or have illnesses or injuries that result in death and even when we have periods of time to prepare for the inevitable, we struggle to cope.

In this case, I spoke with Nikitah the evening before she died; I had no idea she was dying. She had so many dreams; she planned on moving with her husband to New Jersey at some point in the future and was so looking forward to the move. It would have been a fresh start in a new city with new adventures to pursue.

I have been referred to as being 'cold-hearted' because when I was seen in the community or at houses of others I was not a hysterical basket case when Niki's name was mentioned in conversation as a specific memory of her was shared. I will not lie, I cry often, but I cry in private, why would I let my ugly cry-face be seen?

I enjoy thinking about the good times we shared and the memories that remain. I love her in death just as I loved her in life, but my mind needs some free time and I try to limit the sorrow-filled and tearful conversations and might even excuse myself from the conversation if people begin to cry or I think they might cry because they are looking for tissues. Hearing those conversations is not the issue, I love hearing about Nikitah, the issue comes when people begin to cry. I never liked to see people cry as it often results in my crying too, and this is definitely not the time to confront that demon.

I have been going through some of Niki's things and I came upon a box of photos from when she lived at home. The picture right on top of all the others was was of me holding her the day she was born thirty years before. The next thing I knew I was running to the bathroom looking for a place to vomit. I abruptly put the picture back in the box and put it back in the place it sat for so many years; I could not look any further.

Fast-forward about six months and this time I am planning to finally get this done as I remind myself that I must stay focused. I open the box with all of the memories. The first one is the picture of me holding my beautiful little girl and it was bittersweet in that she can no longer breeze through the door and ask me what I am doing but that picture and all the ones that follow it show a beautiful life. Doing my best to stay on point with my trip down Memory Lane, I talk aloud to her and I tell her why I am in her memory box.

Below all of the photos was a corner of what looked like yet another box and as I moved the photos to the side I uncovered a a smaller box she had buried deep inside. I opened the smaller box and found many pictures from her childhood and a picture of a child she was sponsoring at Saint Jude's Research Hospital. Nikitah always tried to help others and if there was money to be donated, she was there to help when her money and time permitted. From a very young age she gave money to Saint Jude's Research Hospital as well as The Shriner's Hospital for Children, and anyone else with a good story and a nice face. She felt that it was important to enhance lives of others, especially children and when she had a few extra dollars, she gave but when money was not there for donations, she helped people. I remember asking why she donated to those specific organizations. She replied, "My childhood was good, mom and I think those kids need to have a chance to live, and see what their lives might be."

By this time, I began thinking of all of the people who do not get to bring healthy children home after their delivery. There are numerous instances where babies do not get to go home and in some cases, when they are sent home, much of their life is spent in a hospital having procedures and treatments. Research is being done to prevent neonatal deaths, sudden infant death syndrome, and a plethora of chronic health issues that effect our children and that train of thought led me in another direction. At that very moment I decided I wanted to help families to get assistance in dealing with these types of situations.

Nikitah came home from the hospital healthy and full of life. She was raised in a good home and had a family that loved her so much. She experienced so many positive things from birthday celebrations, to vacations, time with friends in the pool, and family time to just relax and enjoy life.

As I am writing these words, I feel blessed to have enjoyed thirty plus years with her. I was so proud of the amazing person she had become and the direction her life was going, and I am proud of her as I am sharing her life with you today. She stood strong for what she believed in, had a good sense of self, loved unconditionally with her whole heart, helped others, tutored students to help them make it through school, and even though at times she might be a bit rough around the edges, Nikitah was amazing in so many ways.

CHAPTER 9

LOST AND ALONE

In writing this book, I have had moments of emotional anguish that rendered me totally useless; it has been a bittersweet process for me. In just an hour of writing my emotions have gone from happy thoughts that are a result of a picture of Nikitah that is connected to an amazing memory to sadness and despair connected to the same photo and memory. Pictures of her childhood, her first day of kindergarten, her wedding, or a simple photo of her in the yard often take me on an emotional roller coaster ride. Niki was so special and without her in my life, I often feel so empty. I have my parents, my family, and Dale, but the space they hold in my heart is somehow different then the space that was assigned to Niki.

I know that grief is a normal part of life, but I just was not ready! If God, himself, told me that I needed be ready to accept this pain I would have fought back. I handle pain in my everyday life due to a health condition, but this mental anguish is pure nonsense. There are days I feel really good from a health perspective and I start to get things done. Maybe I am picking up in the living room and something makes me think of Niki so I start thinking about hoe much I miss her and begin to cry. If Dale is home he usually consoles me and I get back on track. When I am home alone and this happens it takes me so much longer to get back to the task at hand, no matter how hard I try.

For at least a year after Nikitah's death I felt so lost and so very alone even with family and friends around me. I have had blocks of time that

I thought I could not get through, especially around holidays, Niki's birthday, her and Mike's wedding anniversary, and times that were important to her. I think of her and what she might be doing if she were still here. Often times, I find myself wondering what her life would look like if she were alive today. Would she be living in New Jersey working as a therapist or teaching Spanish to students in a city school? She had an entire life ahead to look forward to and the fact that it was cut short makes me feel even more lost. It was always my mindset that if you work toward your goal, you will meet it but I am just not so sure anymore.

I apologize for taking you down this dark path with me, but it is where I am some days, not every day, thank God. The intensity of losing Nikitah has been horrific to say the least, and the most challenging thing I have ever experienced. I have my crying spells, actually full blown melt downs before I can regroup and get back on track. Early after Niki's death I was so preoccupied with the why and how of it all. Why did she die so young and how did this happen? How will we all make it without her? While those questions still resurface at times, I try not to let them consume my days like they once did. Her death was attributed to natural causes and identified as a pulmonary embolism. There was simply nothing anyone could have done to change the outcome.

I realized that I needed to allow myself time, and more importantly, quiet time alone to reflect on the life she lived the life that I was so lucky to share with her. That quiet time alone gave me an opportunity to reflect on the life we shared and it gave me the chance to grieve in peace. I spend much of my time during the day keeping myself busy with mundane stuff like household chores making lists for the market, and unnecessary projects. I meditate often and find myself talking to Nikitah like if she were in the room.

I try not to cry in front of people because in some way it makes me feel weak to let others see my vulnerability as my emotions escape while I babble and snot in an almost incoherent way. I speak to her when I am alone when nobody will see me cry or ask questions about why I cry. I talk to Niki every day which often leads to tears. I say things like, *"Niki, do you remember when we did ..... and how much fun we had when,"* and I continue talking out loud to her about all of our amazing memories together. Even as I am writing today I am armed with a box of tissues on the desk in front of me so I am ready to handle the tears as the dam breaks, which it often does with each page I manage to complete. Sometimes I cry through an entire page or two before I can pull myself together!

I know that Nikitah is with me every day. While I cannot see her or physically touch her, I sense that she is here. Sometimes I catch myself laughing over silly things that she liked on television, programs in which I typically would not find humor, programs that now have in some way become funny to me.

She liked some of the older shows that are currently on Antenna TV. These were shows I watched in the eighties before she was born and now I find myself looking for the humor I once saw in them. Niki's eyes were seeing them for the first time and she somehow managed to find humor in them, humor that I once saw when the show fist aired. She enjoyed Three's Company and often said that John Ritter was an awesome actor and that he should be on the big screen not just in a weekly situation comedy. She saw real value in people and that always warmed my soul. Even when she would argue with someone she was able to point out their good traits as we discussed what happened.

When she was younger she often brought up her younger cousin, my sister's daughter, for whom she had admiration and respect. My niece was active in gymnastics and Nikitah always told me, "We might see her in the Olympics some day, Mom, she is good!" She had photos of my niece in her bedroom and sometimes at night I would hear her saying, "I wish we saw each other more, I wish we got along better," and then I would hear her tell her goodnight.

I do that very thing every night before bed and every morning as soon as I am out of the bed; I talk to Niki's picture and say. *"I wish you were here, I miss you so much,"* and I wail like a child that just skinned her knees on concrete in the school yard.

Today, we have pictures of Nikitah throughout our house and I often find myself picking them up and talking to her. Sometimes I remember something awesome that has been tucked in the back of my mind and I talk to her about it and other times I question why this happened and beat myself up for not realizing she was so ill. All those questions do not help, they only tend to bring more tears and I know that even if I had all the answers nothing would be different, she is gone. The days that are filled with those thoughts are painful for me. I am seeing less of them as the time goes by but I realize even though it is lesser than before, the pain will be forever.

The days that I wake up in a horrible, even vial mood the entire day might be really bad for me and sometimes those pictures will get me through it. Other days those very photos may also trigger a storm of tears resulting in a day filled with tears and questions. Those are the days I cry the most and I question how this could happen. I second guess everything I ever did during her life and the *'would have, should have, could have thoughts'* flood my mind. I find myself thinking, "*If only I would have done something differently could it have made a difference?*"

Days that previously were calm and relaxed were now tense and unbearable. Walking through our house and seeing pictures on the walls and end tables that previously brought me happiness and fond memories now brought me pain and tears I thought about taking them off the walls and boxing them up, but my heart told me that doing that would be a disgrace to her memory and all of the joy she brought to my life. Each picture brought a memory of my amazing daughter and had a story attached of something in her life that was important to both of us.

On end tables in the living room were pictures of her in the yard flying kites with her daddy and pictures in the pool with her friends. The walls were adorned with pictures of her wedding with her wonderful husband she chose as a forever mate. The stairway held family memories with photos of a beach trip as well as those taken at the hospital the day they sent her father and I home with our new bundle of joy. Upstairs, the office wall is adorned with artwork she did when she was younger.

All of the bedrooms upstairs shout Niki's name as they all have reminders of her life and the amazing person she was. The bedding and curtains in our bedroom were made by Nikitah and son- in-law, Mike as a Christmas gift and are now coveted possessions and in the event of fire I would risk my own life to save them.

A child who loses his parents is called an orphan and a married person who loses a spouse is referred to as a widow or a widower. There is no term that I am aware of for a parent who loses a child but I think there should be. In the beginning that term would have been Hopeless, however, albeit slow, I feel like things are improving. I think old Mr. Webster missed something important. Maybe there is simply no way to define the emptiness I have been left with, but because it has yet to be defined anywhere, we might all be missing a big piece of the healing process of our grief.

Birth and death are like bookends that hold our life together. The day we are born is the beginning of something special as when we open our eyes we see faces with loving expressions and smiles wanting to hold us, bringing us gifts, and baby talking to us. The day we die is filled with sadness and tears which brings people together once again, but to mourn the loss and pay respects. It is the end of the series referred to as life, that has been carefully packed in between the two ends.

CHAPTER 10

WHO WAS SHE?

I am only including this chapter because some of my strongest memories of her life were fighting to support her through a life that would be ended way too soon. If you find this chapter unappealing, simply move to the next chapter, I felt the need to include this for my own contentment and to help me work through this emotional time. Although developmentally ahead in all areas with exception to speech, Niki was outspoken when she felt the need to be.

From the first words she uttered until the day she died, Niki always said what she was thinking. Although she was typically polite and kind-hearted, Niki shot from the hip and usually did not worry about what people thought, as early as age 4, she spoke what was on her mind and at times would come back to apologize later.

It seems like only yesterday I was teaching Nikitah the alphabet. She was so bright and she loved to learn and she loved even more to be challenged. Many of the activities we engaged in for fun became teachable moments, even though that was not the intention, each of them left imprints in our minds that would forever remain.

Our family has many fond memories of games we played with her and family trips. In an instant she learned to tie her shoes and ride a bike. In what seemed like a blink of the eye she earned three Bachelor's degrees, got married, and moved into a home that she and her husband purchased.

From a very young age, Niki marched to her own drum and was

extremely stubborn. In Kindergarten her teacher wrote a note home saying that she knew Niki would be one of the highest achievers in her class if she was not so concerned about getting everything in perfect order. In First grade Niki came home ranting about how the teacher called a boy a baby because he cried every morning when he came into the classroom. While she was annoyed by the teacher's behavior, Niki's biggest concern was that the boy and his parents lived with his grandmother who passed away the week before while he was in school and the bus dropped him off to a locked house and his grandma did not greet him as she did every other day before.

Later that year, another boy in her class at school who was classified as a slow learner; he was much bigger than all of the other children and according to Niki, he was reprimanded often. He was quickly taken under Niki's proverbial wings. Risking losing her own recess time as a consequence Niki told the teacher, "He is having a bad time and his family is not there for him, so can you leave him alone. Just after Christmas break that same year, the Art teacher ripped Niki's project up because she said, "Niki erased her artwork twice and, we do not have time for that here." Twenty plus years have passed and I still have no idea what she meant when she said there was no time for Niki erasing her own artwork. It was, after all, only Art class and the Art classes I remember were fun and allowed you to explore the world as you knew it and how you fit into that world. Besides, the average first grader is six or seven years old and some of them can barely control the crayons and pastels they are using. These students had the Art Nazi! Is Elementary school not somewhat of a safety net before Middle School or is Elementary School the new Middle School and somehow every first grader in suddenly a fifth grader? Working with school systems myself, I understand the process and arranged for parents to meet at the school office and demand a meeting with the Principal to discuss what was going on within those walls. One other parent showed up and as luck would have it the school went into a 'Code Red' status and a secretary came and told us we would need to leave as they were locking down the school because there was an intruder on the grounds.

The other parent, Mrs. Smitt grabbed her belongings and left. I refused to exit the building because if my child were in jeopardy

I intended to be with her. I stayed right where I was, planted in the hallway right outside of Nikitah's classroom. The teacher had no idea I was outside the classroom door observing her interactions with the class and you can be sure I was taking notes. By the time the Principal called an all clear message on the Public Announcement System and came to find me I had an eight by eleven sheet of paper filled with notes about what the teacher did well and what she was doing that I thought would be damaging to the students. As the Principal and I walked toward his office I shared the list with him and as he perused the list he made a few 'hmmm and ahh' sounds like he just bit into the best or worst candy bar of his life and as we got to the main office he opened the door and allowed me to go inside first. We went directly into his office where he offered me a coffee and we took seats.

Looking down the list he began with, "I see how you might be alarmed by this behavior from a seasoned teacher and I am as well. He told me he was not sure what he could do about it and I felt my blood boiling and in my mind I was thinking, "I know exactly what you should do," but I was trying to be attentive to what he was saying and not come across as one of those obnoxious and overbearing parents. Trying hard to maintain my composure I started with, "Teachers like her do not belong in classrooms with young children," and his response was something to the effect that the teacher had two young adult sons with learning disabilities still living at home resulting in a high stress level and she had been teaching nearly thirty years. He painted a picture of a sad mother who was doing everything she could to raise her own children while giving everything she had left to Niki and the others in her class.

My rebuttal was a suggestion to bring in a co-teacher or to convince her to retire as she had enough time with the school system to get the big bonus package for years of service. I told him, "There are some amazing teachers out there, but tenure allows the worst teachers to remain in the classroom," to which he agreed. He said he would work on a plan and we set up a time to meet the following Monday so I left the office.

A few months later we moved from one town to another, but I let her finish out the school year in the class with which she was familiar. When I brought her to the new school to meet teachers she smiled and said hello, she politely shook each teacher's hand and asked questions of them. When she was satisfied with the answers she said, "When do I start?" She started second grade in the new district and things were so much better. It was pretty much smooth sailing from that point on. The testing at the end of the year showed her IQ to be 128 and the Guidance Counselor identified her as extremely bright and thought she might benefit from the gifted placement, but we discussed it and decided that it would not be a good option.

Her progression through school was steady and she had a few friends she was close to and she took others under her wings trying to give them a positive life; For some reason she felt it was her job to help other children feel good about their lives. In eleventh grade her Guidance Counselor suggested that she apply to Governor's School. It is a competitive program for high-achieving and gifted students to learn on a college campus for six weeks in the summer before their senior year. She came home, application in hand and was anxious to tell me about it. Within a few weeks a letter came in the mail and she hesitantly opened it: "I got into Gov School," she screeched! She was so excited and I was excited for her. Niki looked at a few colleges and toured the campuses. She was given several options and decided that she **was** interested in only of them, sent in her application, and waited. She was fairly sure she would be accepted because her grade point average was a 3.50and there were no disciplinary actions on file, she was never even called to the office for anything.

The waiting was still difficult for her and she checked the mail every afternoon. Finally, the letter came and she opened it, read the first sentence and said, "I start in three weeks!" She read the letter aloud: "We would like to inform you that you have been accepted," the letter listed a start date of August 26.The letter also said an enrollment packet was forthcoming which would further walk her through the process.

She chose to attend the college closest to home for a variety of reasons; less commute time, she could study at home, her friends were nearer to her, and she would be able to be involved in family events. She was a good student and the end of her Baccalaureate career she had earned three Bachelor level degrees. She worked as a Computer

Technician around her class schedule, and worked at a local Steakhouse in the evenings.

It was at college that she met her soul mate, Michael. The two were married on January 19, 2008 and they were so happy. He was an amazing husband to her; they went on trips and enjoyed life as often as they could. She loved the ocean and the beach so much that she and Mike scheduled two consecutive cruises for their honeymoon; they went to the Eastern Caribbean and the Western Caribbean and when they returned home they had pictures and stories about how awesome of a time they had. Niki was certain that she could make Mike love the beach life as much as she did and I believe she may have achieved that goal as the beach seems to be his destination of choice. They planned to move to New Jersey in the future and they took several trips each year to the beach. She always said she felt better breathing in the salt air.

After graduating from college, Niki tutored middle and high school students who were struggling in History, English, and Math, she was a substitute teacher at a local school district for one year after which she returned to school for her Master's Degree. When she died, Nikitah was at the place in her education where she would soon be doing her final internship assignments and would soon be conferred with another degree.

CHAPTER 11

BITTERSWEET MEMORIES

Some readers may find this chapter is not to their liking, so if you decide to skip it and move on, I understand. This chapter has been very therapeutic for me as it helped me work through the memories, both happy and sad. This chapter identifies Nikitah and why she was so special to us.

Nikitah was very inquisitive as a child. She was smart and sassy. She met the milestones rapidly. She walked five or six steps at ten months and the day after her first birthday she walked through our living room and into the kitchen, as if she had been walking forever, picked up her sippy-cup that she had previously left on the floor, and returned to me saying, "All done.". She potty trained herself at fifteen-months-old. She pulled her diaper off, sat on the potty chair I had there for when I would decide to start training her, I guess it was not my choice after all, she did what she needed to do, stood up and clapped her hands. Of course, I praised the behavior and she was so proud. From that day on she no longer wore a diaper and never wet the bed at night. The only milestone she did not meet on time was speech, her R sounds were not coming out as she thought she was saying them and that was a bone of contention.

Although she could speak, she chose not to. As soon as she met the age requirement for enrollment, I signed her into a speech and language preschool at the local university. She loved school even at eighteen months old and could not wait to enter her classroom. Once there, with the group, she usually made her teacher work hard for her money. At times, the teacher asked her to repeat something or identify an item and she would shake her head no and turn away, even at that age, she was an extremely willful child.

She would often indicate her hesitance to do a task with a facial gesture, usually a twisted up nose and a crinkled face. She had a replacement word for the word no in certain situations; the word she chose was BUM in a harsh tone and nobody could ever figure out why. If you asked if she would like more vegetables at dinner she would say, "No," however, if she were asked if she was ready for bed the reply was always, "BUM!"

In the preschool classroom when the teacher asked her to do something, Nikitah usually did it upon the first request just to prove she knew how to complete the task, however, by the second request, she believed it was not important and that is where the replacement word came into play and she made that teacher work hard for every dollar she was paid. That word 'BUM' used to annoy me beyond belief, but as I sit here writing about that particular memory, I would do anything just to hear her say 'BUM' just one more time. She eventually outgrew it, but she remained willful until her last breath. Her and I often spoke about memories I had of her childhood and she would laugh at what we called the 'BUM experience'.

As she grew older she also became more confident. If you asked her do anything for which she had no interest her response would typically be, "Absolutely not." One time some of the kids in her class were planning to get together and asked her to join in on whatever was going on. I did not know this at the time it happened, I was told much later by one of her male friends. He told me her response to that invitation was, "Never," and she further stated,"I plan to go to college and I want my brain cells to be alive and healthy enough to get my degree. She ended up with three degrees and continued learning.

Nikitah loved her family and especially loved spending time with her grandparents and in hindsight, I am so glad I let her spend as much time with them as all the schedules permitted and, truth be told, I sometimes even made up a reason for them to spend time together. I never pushed them to do things with her just as I never kept them apart either. I am so grateful that they were able to build that very special relationship. Niki's Grammy and Pappy, my parents, meant so much to her and she was equally special to them. Her Grandma and Grandpa, her father's parents, were also special to her, but she spent less time with them. When she was young she enjoyed spending time at their house especially when her cousins were there.

Nikitah was very close to her daddy when she was little. He visited her every day until she was nine years old and they had so much fun together playing silly games, taking walks, flying kites, and anything else they could find pleasure in. When she was small she would get her daddy to bake cookies and make chocolate Easter candy with her and it was always a good time until he left for work. He spent numerous hours with her every day before he went to work and sometimes he would come and kiss her goodnight when his shift was done and leave for home. When they were together, the time was hers and her daddy made sure she felt loved. He was in a serious relationship and it was time fore Nikitah to meet his girlfriend so I invited the two of them to our home so Nikitah could meet her with me present. Her dad and his girlfriend sat on the sofa and Nikitah walked over to them a few times and showed them a toy. They interacted with her and things went well. After they left I asked what she thought of her dad's friend. Her response was, "She has kinky hair, can you do that to my hair?" Niki had long straight hair and curls and crimps were not in her future. A few years later, her dad remarried and Nikitah was in the wedding. It was a nice wedding as far as I could tell from Niki's happy smile and her stories of that day.

CHAPTER 12

INHERITANCE, WHY?

When a parent or older person dies you might expect to receive an inheritance, but not when your child passes away. An inheritance is the furthest thought from your mind! Metaphorically speaking, Niki believed in crossing her T's and dotting her I's, she never left anything to be questioned. She left love notes for the people to whom she was closest and I thought that letter completed the circle.

There was a lengthy note to her husband, a note for me, one to her step dad, one to her dad, and notes to her Gram and her Pap, which made me even weepier than I had previously been. When the insurance agent called me shortly after, it was extremely difficult to hear that my child, my thirty-year-old child, thought so far ahead and planned for me in case she was not here. That money still sits in a bank, unused and it is likely that it will eventually make my final house payments or be fed into the foundation I started in her memory.

For several months, my son-in-law, Mike, had been bringing me boxes of Niki's clothes. That in itself is bittersweet in that as I look through them I can envision Niki wearing them, remember shopping with her when they were purchased, or maybe even remember buying them for her as gifts. She always dressed well and she always looked good.

I gave some of those clothes to people I knew could would make use of them and it does my heart good to see the clothes on them. Some of the shirts I can wear now and in some way it makes me feel that she is near on days I put put my arms into the sleeves. Sometimes I cry when I look at pieces she loved so much and other times I feel like she is right here with me in the present moment.

Wearing her clothes and giving them to people who might enjoy them in the same way she did makes me feel, in some way, as if Niki and I have together done one more good deed for others. In some way, that huge void left behind by her death does not seem as big when I am able to help others in her name.

Because Niki enjoyed helping others with her time and monetary donations to non-profit organizations the foundation has been formed in her name to help people with children who are ill and in need of assistance to get to and from appointments as well as other things.

Because these children spend enormous amounts of time in doctors offices and hospitals, living life with any semblance of normalcy often takes a back seat. Siblings are also affected because they miss school to accompany the sick child to appointments when nobody is available to stay with them while parents work or tote them to doctor and hospital appointments. When the foundation began the initial plan was to provide gas and food vouchers to absorb some of the costs involved in making trips to the larger, better equipped hospitals so that children could be afforded care.

The foundation continues to evolve and I am proud to say it continues to support children in the local community who have an illness that compels them to go to a larger hospital specializing in treatment of the illness with which they have been diagnosed. The foundation has also helped with car repairs, and even helped purchase a car for a family to make it to appointments.

The foundation's newest addition is that we currently help children find normalcy by providing for some fun in an otherwise bleak time with gift certificates to child friendly activities that might otherwise not happen. We have given gift cards to fast food restaurants that are in our area and also on the way to hospitals in cities like Philadelphia and Pittsburgh, Pennsylvania. We have given passes for a nearby amusement park and the bounce house so kids can be kids forgetting about doctors and treatments for awhile.

We have made contributions to funeral homes for funerals of

children who parents need a helping hand. Although we are a small non-profit, still in its infancy, we are helping families overcome obstacles in the way of their child's health. Every dollar donated is used to help the children and their families get through the difficult times when dealing with chronic illness. I know Nikitah would approve of the foundation started to help children in her name.

If you should ever find yourself in the Cape May, New Jersey area please stop and visit the Hereford Light House at 111 N. Central Avenue, Wildwood New Jersey and check out the Paver dedication project, where a paver has been placed in memory of Nikitah, see below.

Paver at lighthouse:

In memory of Nikitah Farver 1986-2017 Side by side Or far apart We still feel you in our 🖤

CHAPTER *13*

A NOTE TO THE READER

When I decided to write this book my hope was that someone somewhere would read through the pages and find solace in the words within its covers. I hoped that even just one person would find comfort in knowing that they are not alone in grief and that maybe the thought of somebody else feeling the same horrific feelings of loss and abandonment might in some small way bring a sense of peace in knowing they are not alone in those feelings.

Because grief is not the same for each person dealing with loss, nobody should ever tell you how to grieve or when it is time to stop grieving. The loss of my child was the hardest thing I had experienced to the date of this book's publication and I hope that in some small way the horrific pain with which I struggle will make someone else feel that they can and will get through the terrible loss which they endured and just maybe it will help them want to make it through another day and wake up one more time.

I am living proof that there is a light at the end of the proverbial tunnel. In the beginning I wished that my life would just end but now I thank God that I woke up in the morning. Nikitah would not want my life to stop, in fact, I feel like she watches over me and she experiences my life with me.

This book was a very difficult process for me, the more I wrote, the more I cried and some words were difficult to get onto the page. At one point, I stopped writing and took some time away because the memories were so painful. The happier the memory, the more difficult is was to write about because there was finality in it. My child was gone and no matter how much I prayed or how much I wished to see her again, it would never happen again.

By the last page or two I realized that my beautiful daughter was spared from the pain she might endure if her condition revealed in the autopsy were left untreated. Knowing my daughter like I did, I know in my mind and my heart that she would not have had all of the tests done and, even if she did, she would not have undergone treatment. Her condition would have worsened and she would have been in an enormous amount of pain.

It is said that before we are born our destiny and our end date are predetermined and I am not certain that statement is true. If there is any truth in it, I question why so many unborn children are miscarried, why there are so many innocent lives lost at the hands of others in wars, murders, and abuse situations; I question why people with bright futures ahead are taken from us at a young age. I may never have the answer, but I am sure Nikitah was put on this planet to impact lives. She touched so many lives during her thirty-year -lifespan, most of which were positive and she made many of us want to be better people.

Grief is on a broad spectrum and everyone grieves differently. Who has the right to tell you that it is time to get over it, put on your big boy/girl pants and stop the nonsense, or my all-time favorite, "Just be done with it already!" The heart feels what it feels and most people are clueless when it comes to the effects of death on the mind, heart, and soul of those left behind in this world to deal with the pain and emptiness in our daily lives. If you are reading this book and have not yet experienced death, I am happy for you, but I ask that you be kind to those who have lost a loved on, one day you could be in their shoes and you might need a friend.

When we lost Nikitah, the entire family grieved differently. Each member of our family grieves in their own way. My son-in-law continues to live in the house they made their home but I know he continues to miss her. Work schedules aside, they were together twenty-four hours a day and I am sure he sees her in everything happening at their home. My dad's grief appears to be quiet and personal, although he might break down in front of mom or when he is alone, I am not sure as I am not in their house as much as I was in my younger years.

Nikitah's dad internalizes everything, he always did, so I imagine his grief is hidden somewhere inside of him, but I am certain he is letting it eat him up, My husband only knew Niki for a short time, but it was like he was in her life all along and without him to pick me up when I am down, I can not tell you where I would be today, but since you are reading this book, you already know how I am doing.

Mom cries more often if we are talking about Nikitah or something that triggers a memory of a time with her. I cry for a brief period each morning and every night when I kiss her picture and tell her how much I miss her and love her. I cry throughout the day when I am talking to her, wondering if she hears me or if somehow it simply satisfies my own need to continue the connection I had with her when she was alive. God, I miss her so much

Grief for me has been a tumultuous time in which I often feel as though I am in the middle of a mine field and there are bombs all around me. Some days it feels as though my next step might be the one that brings on the explosion of emotion and tears and some days it does just that. Throughout this book there were full days that I cried like a baby and little was accomplished. I would stop writing and come back after a break. There were times I sobbed so hard that I could not catch my breath and other times when writing about Nikitah made me smile.

There have been times when I am out in the community and someone begins to ask questions that I feel myself begin to tear up so I excuse myself from the area I am in and return after I am composed. Sometimes escaping the situation at hand is the only thing, the way out, which affords me the opportunity to compose my thoughts and rejoin whatever conversation is happening.

At home, Dale often wraps his arms around me when I am crying and even though the pain remains, in some way it makes me feel just a bit better, sometimes just enough to get through the next hour or maybe the rest of the day. Maybe just knowing that I am not as alone as I sometimes feel in this process, helps me cope with the situation. I have my family and we all lost Nikitah but knowing that I do not have the ability to make everything better for them hurts me more that I can tell you.

Grief is often the only way we assuage the pain and agony we suffer after the death of a loved one. Grief is an amazing tool that has been built into our psyche to help us through these trying times. Because each person grieves differently let me say this, "Grieve as long as you feel the need exists. If crying makes you feel better, then cry, but if it is consuming you then you should seek help. There is no manual that tells you when to stop grieving and whatever guidelines may exist out there in cyber-land are often written by someone who believes they have answers for something they have never personally experienced or if they did experience it, experienced it differently. People often feel that they know a little about everything, in my mind, those people are actually the ones who know little, period! Because I need things spelled out right in front of me, I have compiled a list of my thoughts above grieving the loss of a loved one and these may or may not mean anything to you, heck - they might be bathroom reading materials, I do not know at this point!

I refer to these as the ABCs of grief although I only made it to R I guess because it was not necessary for me personally to go any further. I listed them below for you to use as you feel fit. Maybe you want to add your own or maybe you weren't to ignore them all together. Do whatever works for you to get you through this time.

a. Allow yourself to cry: Crying as much as you need until you feel some relief can be good. Crying all day, avoidance such as hiding from the world, not answering phone or texts, pretending nothing happened and a plethora of other ways of dealing with the pain brought on by the death of a loved one are not necessarily good. Although these ways might work for some people, they may not be right for you.

b. Boundaries: Set boundaries, you know what you are willing to discuss and how much you can take so set some boundaries. Nobody has the right to tell you that you should stop grieving or tell you when your grieving process should end. People who do not understand anything about grief say things like... 'Get over it' as if you broke a bone and now it is healed. The words,

"*It is time to stop crying*, should never be said, unless a doctor or therapist is telling you how to deal with the grief and maybe not even then.

c.   Casual: You need relaxed, casual conversations without the typical question and answer sessions that follow a death. You will feel the pain and desperation for as long as you feel it. Do not let anyone tell you when it is time to stop grieving. That is something determined in your heart, not in a book, not in your company's regulations, but in your heart and soul.

d.   Dazed: For me, crying and sobbing while writing this book have been cathartic. Whether you cry silently or babble like a brook, crying is good for your grief and it is a way to cleanse you of the toxins within. For me, it is better to cry alone, because I feel no need to explain my emotions to anyone else, besides who needs to see my ugly scrunched up crying face anyhow. That is a face only a mother could love as I feel the tears coming and then my nose wrinkles up on the end and I can feel each muscle in my face start to become contorted ugh-YUK!

e.   Find your normal: find things to do with people who are not going to ask questions; questions mean answers and answers often mean more tears, tears could mean embarrassment, you get where I am taking this, I hope.

f.   Grief seems to go easier if you take it slow and make it simple. That is just my thought on the subject, for you it might mean being among the masses and keeping busy with involvement and activities simply to go home where you break down and who knows, maybe scream into a pillow.

g.   Look through photos, notes, gift cards, or anything else you have that you might have received from your loved one. These items usually bring some amount of peace and for me they made a world of difference.

h.   Holidays and special occasions such as birthdays anniversaries, summertime, wintertime, and any other day that had special meaning might cause you to be weepy and open the flood gates to lots of tears and many breakdowns. It might be your loved ones birthday or the date of their death but either way, it means something to you and it helps you to heal.

i. Incredible, Icy, and Impeccable: Write a note to your loved one filled with love and memories putting your personal spin on it, I might say something like, do you remember the day we ice skated and all the fun we had? It was so cold my toes were icy cold and you laughed at me who got me laughing and then I fell and you laughed harder. You let me borrow your scarf and I was rocking it, you always did have impeccably good fashion sense. Write these notes often because each memory has a way of making you feel better because you are getting your feelings out. In some way this brings closure because you can say the I love you, I miss you, I only wish I knew, the would have- should have-and could haves will all spew onto the paper which is empowering and gives you strength to live another day.

j. Jaded: You are likely jaded (tired and dulled by the emotional toll this death has brought on you. You need to find a way to let loose and feel good again. Feel free to come up with the letters from K to Z as they are for your own benefit.

k. Key: The key to making it through the grieving process is to learn the ways to cope on a daily basis. No matter how hard you try, you will never be able to assign a number to your grief. So if someone asks you, "On a scale of one to ten…," you tell them grief is not quantifiable and you will not rate it and that you want to talk about something else.

l. Lazy: Remember that sometimes having a lazy day can let you recharge and get the healing started again. Take a day or two off when you need it and think about where you are and the progress you are making.

m. Meaningful: I need to find the purpose for my life so it will have meaning. For so many years, my purpose in life was to be Nikitah's mom.

n. Nervous: For a period of time after receiving the phone call about death I was nervous every time the phone rang and that is normal so I must convince myself it will be okay and I answer the call

o. Objective: Try to remain objective while people are asking questions about how, why, what happened. Try to remain calm and state your point in a kind manner. People are typically.

p. Peaceful: Try to find a time and place to have peace and tranquility, time for you to take a deep breath, relax, and reflect on life before this death.

q. Quality vs. Quantity: try to focus on quality of the relationship as opposed to the quantity of time spent together.

r. Rest: Be certain you are getting plenty of rest as grieving can be very tiring and the sleep will help you be ready for whatever tomorrow brings your way. It is sort of like recharging your battery so you can keep going like that silly pink bunny walking around with his drum. Remember, grieve the way you need to, not the way you are told to by anyone else, including me!

**Please feel free to add to this or if it helps you, rip out the pages.

It is my personal belief that life and love are truly forever. I further believe that there are two states of being; there is the state in which we exist today and there is also a transitional state where we live a huge part of the afterlife and decisions are made about where we will spend eternity. It is in this state where we are free from the angst of our earthly struggles and live a pain-free existence and a joyous life.

I believe that upon our death the soul transitions to that next state or level of being and that could be where judgment occurs. Who knows, maybe Saint Peter is there with the list of things we did in our lives or we might have already met him and we just did not realize it at the time.

I am not trying to change your beliefs in one way or the other, but my belief is that Jesus might very well walk among us and he might even take on the form of a beggar, homeless person, or a thief, or even a prisoner, so treating people with respect and dignity are of utmost importance to me. I help people who need help, give money to charitable causes, and have even taken people into my home, giving them a place to stay, when they hit hard times, and who knows when I might be tested and my choices might just help me pass the final exam. The Bible maps out the paths our lives should take to gain entrance to Heaven after we die and maybe more people should be reading the good book, just a thought. At this time I want to take a moment to personally thank you for reading this book. It is my sincere hope that this will have been of some use for you, even if only to level the short leg on your kitchen table. The last pages of this book will include a letter to Nikitah and more photos of her life. She was full of energy and I only wish you knew her as I did. She will be forever missed!

Things I often say to Nikitah when I am here missing her so much have been written into a short letter.

LETTER TO NIKITAH
Chaloops, (my nickname for her)

I would do anything just to see your smile or touch you one more time. I miss you so much. Not a day goes by that I do not think of you and wish you were here. I hope you can hear me when I tell you good morning, goodnight, or how much I miss you.

You were my reason to live, you were my good luck charm, my muse, my energy source, and whether or not you knew it or not, I wished many times I was more like you. I never knew anyone as smart and amazing as you and that is why I called you when I had questions or could not figure something out.

I wanted a baby so badly and I prayed on it for a year or better. I was so excited the day the doctor told me I was pregnant with you. The day you were born was the best day of my life. Having you in my life was a wonderful blessing and each day was often a new experience for both of us; I was growing as a parent and you were growing as my child.

Your progression through life in the physical world was steady and constant. There were a few hurdles along the way and some hoops to jump through but you tackled them head on and survived made it through each one! You were a strong willed young lady who always had a good sense of direction and you were always focused on your goal.

I wish I could be more like you; you stood for what you believed in and held your ground. You loved without condition and gave with your whole heart. I am still confused about why you were taken at age thirty and I was left here in a weak state of health. I wish I could have taken your place and you could have lived your life to its fullest. You had so much left to do.

While I know you have physically left this world I believe that you are with me every day, I can feel you here and I can sense you in things that I do and say. I wish I had more time with you here in the physical life but there is some security in knowing we will be reunited when it is my final day comes and I will join you.

When I say something that I would not typically say that sounds like your words or your sense of humor, I am certain you are with me. Sometimes I watch half or more of a television program you watched when you were at home before I realize I am watching it. The oddity there is that I find myself laughing at the absurd stuff happening on the screen and sometimes even watch the next episode. Who knows? Maybe that is my way to honor you or maybe you are with me those days. I guess you did rub off on me some.

I wonder if you hear me when I talk to you. I hope you do because that means you know how much I love you. I miss you so much and I love You! Maybe I did not tell you often enough how much I admire you. Your tenacity, willingness to help those who needed you most, bravery, and your inner strength have always amazed me. Because of you I am a better person.

We learned together as we made it through the hills and valleys of life. Your fortitude taught me so much about living and your compassion taught me to love without limits.

When it is my time to join you I know you will be there waiting to bring me into my next life. I miss you so much and as I am writing this, tears are streaming down my cheeks and falling to the keyboard, but I guess maybe you already know that.

Until we meet again my sweet child,
Love, Mom

Writing about such painful subject matter as the death of Nikitah has been so extremely difficult and there have been many bumps in the road, sometimes they were boulders that I thought I would never get around.

I want to share with all of my readers just how amazing my family has been throughout this process. They have given me space and time to grieve in my own way and they continue to support me each day.

I want to thank Dale, my husband, for holding me everytime tears erupted out of nowhere and for being by my side every step of the way. I want to tell everyone how amazing Niki's husband, Mike, has been. He was an amazing husband to Niki and he met her every need. She spoke often of how terrific he was and how happy he made her. He continues to be a good daddy to their two fur babies and he remains an important part of our family. My parents are awesome in that while they are dealing with their own pain from the loss of a grandchild, they continue to move forward and love all the entire family.

We recently went to New Jersey and spent time on the pier that was one of Nikitah's favorite places and while it was difficult, we all made it through it. My mind kept flashing back to happy days when I put Niki on the very rides I was putting my grandchildren on. The tears would come and go. I felt as though Niki was probably right there with me the entire time and maybe that is what got me through it.

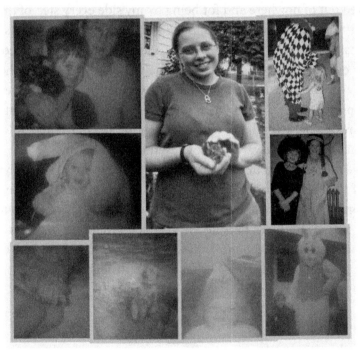

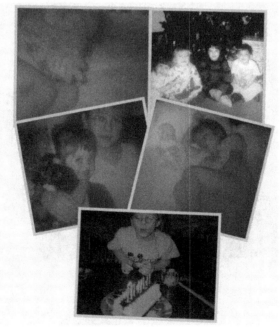

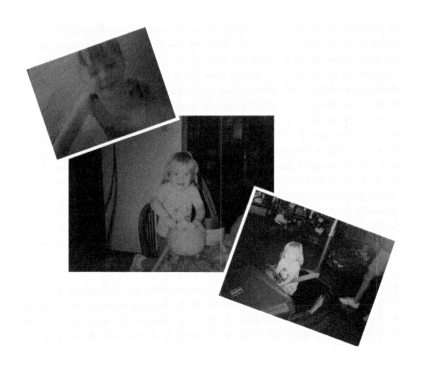

.

Printed in the United States
By Bookmasters